RUSSIAN
SOUVENIRS

**DECORATIVE PAINTING
ON WOOD**

WOOD-CARVING

LACQUERS

CLAY TOYS

CERAMICS

**EMBROIDERY AND LACE.
PRINTED KERCHIEFS**

BONE-CARVING

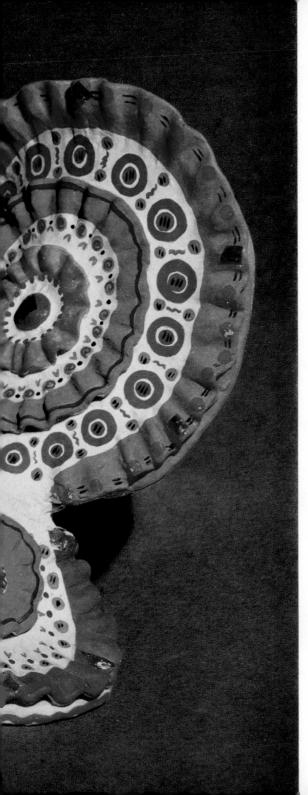

STONE-CARVING

METALWORK

PORCELAIN AND FAIENCE

GLASS AND CRYSTAL

RUSSIAN SOUVENIRS

Aurora Art Publishers

Leningrad

Compiled
by **M. CHEREISKAYA**

Designed
by **D. PLAKSIN**

P $\frac{80104\text{-}929}{023(01)\text{-}78}$ 16-77

DECORATIVE AND APPLIED FOLK ART,
WHICH IS AN INALIENABLE PART
OF SOVIET SOCIALIST CULTURE,
EXERTS AN ACTIVE INFLUENCE ON THE
SHAPING OF THE PEOPLE'S ARTISTIC TASTES,
ENRICHES PROFESSIONAL ART
AND THE POSSIBILITIES OF INDUSTRIAL DESIGN...
HIGH ARTISTIC MERITS DISTINGUISH LACQUER
MINIATURES, ENAMEL AND LACE ITEMS,
BONE- AND STONE-CARVINGS, CERAMICS
AND OTHER WARES PRODUCED AT RENOWNED
ART CENTRES WHICH KEEP ALIVE
TIME-HONOURED CREATIVE PRINCIPLES
AND WORK PROCESSES.

From the decree of the Central Committee of the CPSU
On Artistic Folk Handicrafts (*Pravda*, February 27, 1975)

DECORATIVE PAINTING ON WOOD

Kovernin district (Gorky region) was famous for its artistic handicrafts. Most of the local inhabitants had since olden times been engaged in manufacturing painted wooden tableware and the turned toy, in carving wooden spoons and painting icons.

Khokhloma wares (so named after the village on the Volga) are profoundly national and highly original in their colour combinations, ornamental motifs and in the technology of their manufacture. The item is first fashioned from a chunk of wood, the unpainted "whiteness" is primed, steeped in drying oil, and aluminium powder is then rubbed in by hand. Thus processed, the surface turns "silver". An improvised decorative pattern in oil paints is then laid on with free strokes of the brush. The painted items are given several coats of a special varnish and then fired in a furnace where the high temperature turns the aluminum powder under the varnish coating into glittering "gold" and tempers the painted décor into a riot of colours. One of two methods are used to paint the item—"overlay" painting (a delicate open-work design is applied with strokes of the brush over the background layer), and "backdrop" painting (a golden silhouette drawing against a black or coloured background). Some of the Khokhloma designs hark back to ancient Russian ornamental motifs.

The Russian *matrioshka*, which has come to be the national souvenir, is well known and very popular in many countries of the world. This unpretentious toy is as yet quite young: it made its first apprearance in 1900 at the World Fair in Paris. *Matrioshkas* are produced in Semionov, Zagorsk and other towns. The soft wood (usually lime-tree) is turned on a lathe; the product is then "dressed" in bright *sarafans* and kerchiefs with a pattern of roses and forget-me-nots painted in aniline dye or oil.

Objects from Gorodets (a town in Gorky region) have more of the national tradition in their aspect and colouration. In the nineteenth century many of the villages along the Uzola river in the province of Nizhni Novgorod were engaged in the manufacture of distaff bases adorned with colourful painting on themes from merchant, peasant and urban life. At present Gorodets painting, whose salient feature is an unpainted background, is used in decorating children's furniture, caskets and chopping boards. Large succulent floscules rhythmically disposed over the item's surface merge into picturesque garlands and bouquets. In the centre of the composition are fantastic birds and steeds which form an intricate ornamental pattern.

The production of turned and painted wares in Polkhovsky Maidan (Gorky region) is a relatively young handicraft which traces its beginnings to the early twentieth century. It was only in the 1920s, though, that the local painting finally came into its stylistic own. Aniline dyes began to be used in the 1930s—they are less labour-consuming than oil paints. Polkhovsky-Maidan decorative painting is done with local colours (scarlet, yellow, blue) which when applied in consecutive layers produce very intensive tones inside a contour designated in Indian ink. Vivid patches of vegetal ornamentation fuse organically with the pictorial elements of the composition—a house, a sun or a river. The disparity between the elements that often ensues is characteristic of folk art and lends the composition a special decorative quality.

←

1 Khokhloma decorative roundel:
The Firebird. 1970
Painted by N. Ivanova and N. Salnikova

2 Khokhloma *postavets* containers. 1970
Painted by V. Grachiov

3 Khokhloma soup set. 1971
   Painted by N. Salnikova, N. Ivanova, N. Morozov
   and A. Savinova

→
4 Khokhloma beer set. 1970
   Painted by N. Ivanova and N. Salnikova

5 Khokhloma decorative panel. 1960s. Detail
Painted by S. Veselov

6 Decorative plate. 1975
Painted by L. Bespalova
Gorodets folk painting

7, 8 Chopping boards. 1973
   Painted by F. Kasatova
   Gorodets folk painting

9 Semionov *matrioshkas.* 1973

10—13 Russian souvenirs. 1970s
Polkhovsky-Maidan folk painting

14 Polkhovsky-Maidan toy: *Horse and Cart*. 1971
Painted by P. Sinteriov

WOOD-CARVING

Sergiyev Posad (now the town of Zagorsk) has from the seventeenth century been known as a major producer of the Russian wooden toy. Simultaneously the craft also flourished in the village of Bogorodskoye, 27 kilometres from Sergiyev Posad.

The Bogorodskoye toy is made of the softer species of wood—lime-tree, asp and alder. A three-sided block is carved manually with shallow cuts of a chisel and knife into the desired shape, which is always simple, generalized and highly expressive. The Bogorodskoye toy is light-hued, the colour of natural, unpainted wood. Especially popular and characteristic is the "motive" toy—hens pecking grain; a bear and a peasant alternately striking an anvil with a hammer; peasants sawing firewood. The craftsmen's favourite personage is Mishka the Bear. In Soviet times the Bogorodskoye toy's range of themes widened considerably in that the artisans concerned turned to subjects taken from contemporary life—in the 1930s the *Cheliuskin* epic, then the events of the Great Patriotic War, and later still the exploration and conquest of space. The Zagorsk toy comes in a large variety of subjects. Unlike the Bogorodskoye toy, it is painted. In the old days the Bogorodskoye masters usually carved the toys, which were then painted in Zagorsk.

The Khotkovo Factory of Carved Items (Moscow region) produces souvenirs based on the rich folk art traditions of Russian wood-carving. Their style and technique stem from the Abramtsevo-Kudrino tradition, which began with the organization in 1884 in the country estate of Abramtsevo (Moscow region) of a joiner's workshop. This workshop was headed by the paintress Polenova, a member of the so-called "Abramtsevo circle" which brought together the best Russian artists, and a collector of folk art. The designs which she drew for the wood-carvers were based on the motifs and techniques peculiar to the different kinds of relief carving of the North. Among those working here in the early twentieth century was the talented master Vornoskov from the village of Kudrino, who is considered one of the creators of the Abramtsevo-Kudrino style. Completing its evolution in Soviet times, this style organically united the techniques of folk carving with the newest methods of wood-processing. Deep cuts are made in the wood, and these produce matt patterns which stand off beautifully against the sheen of the item's polished surface.

Birch-bark items have long been produced near the northern town of Veliky Ustiug in villages situated along the banks of the Shemoksa river. The outer, flexible layer of the bark of the birch-tree is an extremely adaptable material from which the Shemoksa craftsmen produced all manner of boxes, baskets and plates. An openwork pattern is traced on the bark with a blunt awl, then cut out with a sharp knife. To accentuate the pattern a sheet of tin foil is often glued onto the inside of the box or basket. Today birch-bark art items are produced in many areas of the Russian North, primarily in the Arkhangelsk region.

15 Loving cup. 1969
By P. Sinitsyn
Khotkovo wood-carving

16 Vase. 1974
By G. and N. Simankin
Khotkovo wood-carving

←

17 Scoop. 1969
   By V. Balashov
   Khotkovo wood-carving

18 Birch-bark casket. 1972

19 Carved birch-bark baskets. 1972
By A. and V. Petukhov

→
20 Bogorodskoye wooden toy:
General Bear. 1975
By Ye. Sidorov

21 Bogorodskoye wooden toy:
Bear Bending Yokes. 1973
Carved after the original of I. Stulov

22 Bogorodskoye wooden toy:
Too Much Hospitality. 1970
By M. Smirnov

LACQUERS

The first artistic objects of lacquered papier-maché with miniature decorative painting were produced at the end of the eighteenth century in the village of Fedoskino of Moscow province. The lacquer crafts of Palekh, Mstera and Kholui had their beginning after the October Revolution, when the manufacture of lacquered items on the Fedoskino model was started in these ancient icon-painting centres. The former icon-painters brought into the new art the techniques, the compositional devices and the refined colour schemes of ancient Russian painting.

The papier-maché item is coated with several layers of dense ground (putty), each layer being subjected to drying, leveling and polishing. The item is then covered with a black varnish and ornamented with miniature painting which is fixed by several layers of colourless varnish and polished to a mirror finish.

The craftsmen of the Fedoskino Factory do their painting on black lacquer in three to four layers of oils, whereas the artists of Mstera (Vladimir region), Palekh and Kholui (Ivanovo region) use tempera for the purpose, hence the tonal purity and transparency of the colour layer in their works. The pride of the Fedoskino school is its decorative painting in transparent glazes on a base consisting of tinsel gold leaves, nacre or metal powder, as a result of which the colours seem to glow from within.

The artists of Palekh, Mstera and Kholui favour folktale and *bylina* motifs and historical subjects, at the same time devoting much effort to the modern theme which is treated in a symbolic manner combining fantasy with reality.

One of the elements of Palekh art which tends to heighten the decorativeness of its wares is the black background of its painting, whereas the artists of Mstera always place their personages in a meticulously rendered polychromatic landscape.

The distinguishing features of Kholui miniatures are that their compositions are built of enlarged details, and their images, based as they are on sketches done from nature, are more material, more concrete.

Painted metal trays are produced in the village of Zhostovo (Moscow region). The origins of this branch of folk art date back to the late eighteenth century, when decorative metal trays first made their appearance in St. Petersburg and in the Ural region. From about the middle of the nineteenth century they spread to the Moscow region and there quickly came to the forefront in the field of artistic metal.

Nowadays the trays of Zhostovo are stamped on electric presses irrespective of form or size. Processing the trays with ground and varnish is by and large similar to the technology used for processing papier-maché items. The Zhostovo artists use oil paints heavily diluted by linseed oil. Usually the painting is done on the traditional black background, though other colours—red, blue or green—are not too rare either. Sometimes aluminum or bronze powder is mixed into the paint, and this lends it a silvery or goldish hue.

25 Tray: *Bunch of Roses*. 1974
Painted by G. Podymova
Zhostovo folk painting

26 Tray: *Tea-drinking*. 1972
Painted by N. Litipov in imitation
of the original by A. Suvorov
Zhostovo folk painting

27 Kholui decorative panel: *Troika*. 1973
Painted by A. Musatov after the original
of V. Belov

28 Brooches. 1970s
    Palekh, Kholui and Mstera folk painting

29 Palekh casket. 1975
    Painted by V. Lebedev

30 Palekh casket: *The Bogatyrs*. 1973
    Painted by T. Siviakova

31 Mstera decorative panel:
The Firebird. 1973
Painted by P. Sosin

32 Palekh decorative panel:
    Frog Tsarevna. 1975
    Painted by N. Malinkin

33 Palekh powder-case:
Down by the Riverside. 1974
Painted by N. Lopatin

CLAY TOYS

Dymkovo, a small village in the environs of Viatka (now the city of Kirov), had by the mid-nineteenth century become a major centre of manufacture of the clay toy. It is an art which has survived to this day and continues to flourish. The Dymkovo toy of fired unglazed clay is widely known outside the Soviet Union. It makes a splendid bit of décor for the modern interior, bringing as it does into the home a radiant and festive atmosphere.

The material of the toys is the local red clay with an admixture of sifted sand. The hand-moulded figurines are dried, burned and painted in tempera on a bleached surface. The coloristic pattern of the painting is based on the contrasting of blue and yellow, crimson and green, black and white. To strengthen the decorative effect the painting is supplemented by ornamental rings, ovals or tiny squares of copper leaf glued on for brilliance. The figurines, be they human beings, animals or birds, are always treated in a humorous vein: water-carrying girls, women of fashion, nursemaids are endowed with precisely observed and deliberately overplayed characteristics. Three-headed billy goats, horsemen, steeds, turkeys, penny-whistles of every description, all bring to mind the gay atmosphere of fairs and folk festivals and all appeal to the eye for the unique character of their generalized forms and decorative qualities.

The Filimonovo toy (from the village of Filimonovo, Tula region) differs widely from its Dymkovo counterpart. It is more archaic in form and less colourful in décor: the decorative painting is done directly on the burnt clay (without the white background) in characteristic varicoloured strips of aniline dyes blended on an egg base. Highly generalized and very expressive are the Filimonovo figurines of long-necked horses and their riders.

The Kargopol toy (Kargopol, Arkhangelsk region), which grew out of a peasant handicraft in the nineteenth century, was revivified in the mid-1960s largely thanks to the efforts of Babkina, a talented craftswoman and the last remaining custodian of this traditional art.

Today there is a pottery workshop at Kargopol engaged in the production of toys: penny-whistles, human, animal and bird figures, simple compositions. The Kargopol clay toy is noted for its archaic imagery, naive modelling and its primitive but expressive decorative painting of two or three hues.

The penny-whistles produced in the village of Abashevo (Penza region) have little of the toy about them. Most of these figurines of animals and birds hark back to an ancient and highly developed culture handed down from one generation of craftsmen to the next. These reify in perfect plastic form the age-old poetic images of man's patrons and protectors. Majestic in spite of their small size, their decorative painting done in local colours, they are extremely impressive. The red, black and green tones of the toys are enlivened by gold or silver paint.

34 Dymkovo clay toys:
Nanny and *Smart Lady*. 1960s
By Z. Penkina and Z. Kazakova

35 Dymkovo clay toy: *Round Dance.* 1974
    By L. Falaleyeva

36 Dymkovo clay toy: *Troika*. 1964
    By Z. Penkina

37 Dymkovo clay toy: *Steeds.* 1970s
By Ye. Koss-Denshina and L. Falaleyeva

38 Kargopol toys. 1972
   By U. Babkina

39 Abashevo penny-whistles. 1972
By T. Zotkin

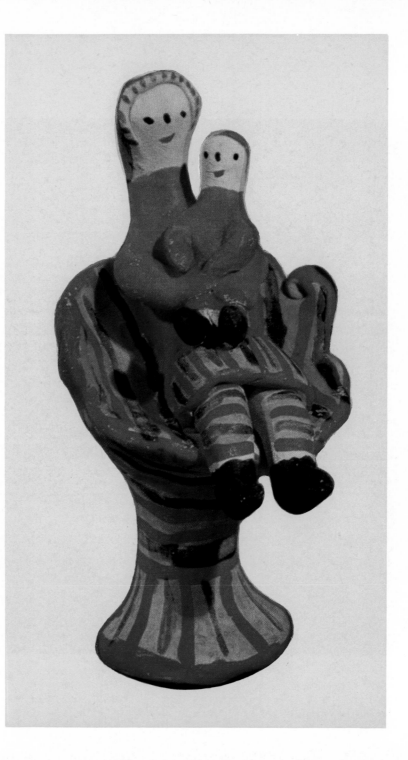

40 Filimonovo clay toy:
   Mother and Baby. 1973
   By Ye. Karpova

41 Abashevo penny-whistles. 1972
   By I. Ziuzenkov

→
42 Filimonovo clay toy: *Horseman*. 1973
   By Ye. Karpova

→
43 Filimonovo clay toy: *Bears*. 1960s

CERAMICS

The Gzhel district, which lies about 60 kilometres south-east of Moscow, has long been famous for its clay deposits. The main features of the local pottery craft, which harks back to very ancient times, evolved in the sixteenth and seventeenth centuries. The majolica tableware of Gzhel came to be very popular in the eighteenth century, when Gzhel was one of the most important centres of ceramics production in Russia. Its very original *kvass*-jugs, *kumgans* (ewers), dishes and inkstands were produced from high-grade light clay, the décor being painted over the moist enamel in yellow (antimony), cobalt blue, green (copper), black, and violet (manganese) colours. The diversified ornamentation of the items was in perfect harmony with their complex thematic pictures; often the vessels were also adorned with a sculptured décor, which was painted in the same colour scheme. Beginning with the late eighteenth century Gzhel began to produce half-faience items coated with a colourless transparent glaze and decorated with painting in cobalt blue. Later, in the first quarter of the nineteenth century, the manufacture was organized from imported clay of Gzhel porcelain, whose distinctive feature is bright floral ornamentation.

Today the Turyghino Ceramics Factory (Moscow region) produces faience tableware and souvenir statuettes in the Gzhel tradition. The forms of the items and the character of the décor are reminiscent of Gzhel semi-faience with underglaze painting in cobalt blue.

Another ancient pottery centre is the town of Skopin (Riazan region). The special properties of the local clay—its very light hue and its plasticity—led to the development in Skopin of the singular decorative technique of glazing the items in very effective yellow, green and brown hues. The Skopin craftsmen put out a wide variety of tableware items: bowls, jugs, handwashers, pots, penny-whistles. Especially popular in the second half of the nineteenth century were Skopin glazed vessels in the shape of fantastic animals and birds.

In the long years of its existence the pottery craft of Skopin has undergone significant changes: to comply with modern tastes the figured ceramic items are now made much smaller in size. The souvenirs, decorative figurines and vessels of Skopin are nowadays cast into gypsum moulds or shaped by hand.

44 Skopin earthenware jug. 1953
By M. Pelionkin

45 Skopin earthenware jugs. 1973, 1974
By A. Rozhko and N. Nasonova

46 Skopin earthenware *kvass*-jug. 1963
By Yu. Logvin

→
47 Skopin earthenware jug. 1963
By M. Peltonkin

←

48 Gzhel majolica jug. 1960
    By L. Azarova

49 Gzhel majolica *kvass*-jug. 1966
    By L. Azarova

50 Gzhel majolica tea set. 1964
    By L. Azarova

51 Gzhel majolica group:
A Peasant Family. 1963
By L. Azarova

52 Gzhel majolica figurines. 1960s
By L. Azarova and N. Kvitnitskaya

EMBROIDERY AND LACE. PRINTED KERCHIEFS

Embroidery, one of the most widespread branches of Russian decorative and applied art, is used to adorn everyday and festive clothes, and many household items as well. The art of Russian embroidery originated ages ago. It is an art that reflects the artistic experience of the people and witnesses to the craftsmanship and talent of many generations. The embroidery of Russian needlewomen is unmatched for its harmonious colour combinations, the beauty of its patterns and the variety of techniques employed.

The Krestsy district of the Novgorod region is known for its white linen wares which are embellished with white openwork embroidery of a geometric pattern—the so-called Krestsy stitch. This pattern, which consists of a complex interlacing of rhombs, rosettes and stars on a background of large-size netting, is extremely subtle and elegant. The stylistic peculiarities of the Krestsy stitch were fully developed by the beginning of the twentieth century, and the craftswomen of today continue to uphold the tradition in their needlework.

The Tarussa Factory of Artistic Embroidery (Kaluga region) widely uses in its output the device of "coloured twining", which had been popular with the needlewomen of Smolensk, Tver, Kaluga, Riazan and Orel provinces since time immemorial. The Tarussa craftswomen do their embroidery on netting which is intertwined with coloured threads, red as a rule. Against this red openwork background the white pattern of geometric figures or flat depictions of animals and human beings stands out sharply.

Russian bobbin lace, whose origins go back to the eighteenth century, is world renowned. The historic and economic centre of lace-making in Russia is Vologda, one of the oldest cities of the Russian North. In fact, the bobbin lace of the North is known throughout the country as Vologda lace. The main centres of lace-making today are the city of Vologda, many districts of the Vologda region, and likewise the towns of Sovietsk (Kirov region) and Yelets (Lipetsk region). Each of these places has developed its own specific style of the subtle and painstaking art. The ornamentation of modern lace items is faithful to the old traditions; Soviet lace weavers have developed those traditions and enriched them with new motifs.

Pavlov Posad is a very old little town 40 kilometres from Moscow. In the seventeenth and eighteenth centuries it was a major trading village and a centre of textile production. In the nineteenth century it came to be widely known for its printed kerchiefs with a bright floral motif. Large red roses with emerald-green leaves, miniature vegetal ornaments, wreaths and garlands of flowers were strewn impressively over a white, green or black background. Stylistically the Pavlov Posad kerchiefs share an affinity with Zhostovo trays. They have long been an inalienable part of Russian life; many major artists were fond of painting them—Repin, Surikov, Kustodiev, for example. Today the Moscow Kerchief Production Association (in the town of Pavlov Posad) produces kerchiefs from woollen, half-woollen, half-silk and cotton fabrics.

53 Embroidered border of a towel. 1970
By M. Gumilevskaya
The Tarussa Factory of Artistic
Embroidery, Kaluga region

54 Doily. 1953
By V. Grigoryeva
The "Yelets Lace" Factory,
Yelets

55 Doily. 1967
By Z. Varaksina
Lace Factory, Kirov

→

56 Embroidered border of the towel
"Little Roosters". 1972
By A. Kislina
The "Krestsy Stitch" Factory, Novgorod region

57, 58 Woollen shawls. 1950s
By Z. Olshevskaya
Pavlov Posad, Moscow region

→
59, 60 Designs on woollen kerchiefs. 1960s
By E. Regunova and N. Slashcheva
Pavlov Posad, Moscow region

BONE-CARVING

The artistic processing of bone is an old Russian tradition. Carved bone items from the North enjoyed a world reputation as far back as the seventeenth century. Especially widely known was the output of the bone-carvers of Kholmogory (Arkhangelsk region): their vases, caskets, tobacco-boxes and wine-cups were in heavy demand throughout the eighteenth century, when the art was at its peak. It was then that the basic Kholmogory carving technique came into being—a combination of an openwork background with thematic scenes in relief, colour engraving and inlays. Eighteenth century items of carved bone had a strongly pronounced decorative aspect; today they are on display at the Armory, Moscow, the Hermitage, Leningrad, and other museums.

The Lomonosovo Bone-carving Factory of our day (the village of Lomonosovo, Arkhangelsk region) puts out a wide range of caskets, cigarette-cases, paper-cutters, vases, and various items of decorative wear—pendants, beads, earrings. The materials used are walrus tusk, cachalot tooth and ordinary animal bone. The miniature reliefs adorning the items are often thematic compositions on various aspects of the way of life and natural scenery of the North. The Tobolsk Bone-carving Factory (Tiumen region) was organized on the basis of the widespread bone-carving craft which originated in those parts in the second half of the nineteenth century thanks to the efforts of Znamensky, a Siberian artist. The Tobolsk masters produce remarkable miniature sculptures and multifigure compositions from a very precious material—mammoth ivory which is unearthed from time to time in digs on the territory of Western Siberia. Cachalot teeth are used to produce small-size works of plastic art, and walrus ivory serves as the material for thematic compositions.

63 Walrus ivory figurine:
Lassooing a Deer. 1968
By N. Butorin
The Lomonosovo Bone-carving Factory,
Arkhangelsk region

64 Walrus ivory figurine:
   Reindeer Herdsman. 1973
   By D. Khorishchenko
   The Tobolsk Bone-carving Factory,
   Tiumen region

65 Walrus ivory vase. 1969
   By N. Butorin
   The Lomonosovo Bone-carving Factory,
   Arkhangelsk region

STONE-CARVING

The origins of the stone-carving art in Russia go a very long way back in time, down to the epoch when the Russian state itself was still in the making. Works by Russian masters are extant that date to the eleventh and twelfth centuries and are outstanding for their beauty and the perfect craftsmanship of their execution. Such, for example, are the details of the interior décor in the Cathedral of St. Sophia of Kiev, the stone reliefs in the shape of animals, birds and flowers on the walls of the Cathedral of St. Demetrius in Vladimir, the fretted arched frieze of the Church of the Intercession on-the-Nerl, and the fretted window surroundings of white stone adorning the Palace of Facets (Granovitaya Palata) in the Moscow Kremlin.

The first lapidary works in the country was founded during the reign of Peter the Great in Peterhof (now Petrodvorets, a suburb of Leningrad); in 1726 a lapidary and grinding factory was inaugurated in Ekaterinburg (now Sverdlovsk), and in the last third of the eighteenth century—the Kolyvan works in the Altai territory. Right up to the turn of the nineteenth and twentieth centuries the stone-working industry was completely lacking in machines and all the processing was done by hand.

In the eighteenth century Russian masters executed the architectural details for the Winter and Marble Palaces in St. Petersburg, the Great Kremlin Palace in Moscow and other palace construction projects. Huge decorative vases in the shape of tall flat bowls were produced in large numbers; cut out of Ural minerals—jasper, lapis lazuli, malachite and marble—and embellished with ormolu details, they are today the pride of many a Soviet museum collection. At the beginning of the nineteenth century the monumental creations of the stone-carving art gave way to smaller items: desk sets, candlesticks, caskets, signets, brooches and cameos. The close of the century saw a rising interest in animalistic sculpture.

Today new plants in the Urals, the Altai territory, the Arkhangelsk region and other parts of the country are reviving the past glory of coloured stone.

The best reputation in the field belongs to the items produced by the factories of the "Russian Semi-Precious Stones" Trust. The Sverdlovsk plant, successor to the Ekaterinburg Lapidary Works, manufactures items from the hard species of minerals (orlets, jasper, nephrite) and jewellery with inlays of Ural semi-precious stones. The plant's toilet sets, jewellery boxes, trays and vases are extremely attractive for the elegance of their forms, the semi-transparency of the stone, the natural beauty of its texture which is underlined by polishing, and the play of light on the facets. The ornamental qualities of Russian semi-precious stones stand out especially well in combination with gold and silver.

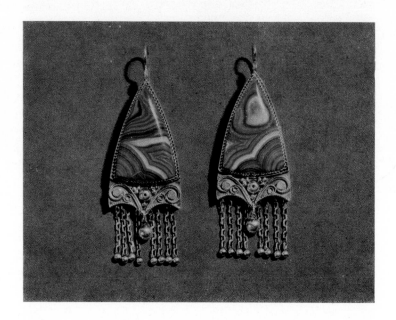

←
66 Malachite box. 1970s
   By V. Bakulin

67, 68 Personal ornaments. 1970s
   By L. Ustyantsov and N. Statsenkova
   The "Russian Semi-precious
   Stones" Factory, Sverdlovsk

69 Malachite box. 1970s
By S. Budanov

70 Toilet set in onyx. 1970
    By Yu. Paas-Alexandrova
    The "Russian Semi-precious
    Stones" Factory, Sverdlovsk

71 Jasper box and hornstone bottle. 1971, 1972
By V. Molchanov and Ye. Vasilyev
The "Russian Semi-precious
Stones" Factory, Sverdlovsk

METALWORK

The artistic working of metals is one of the oldest branches of the decorative and applied arts at which Russian masters were adept as long ago as the Kievan Rus period (ninth to eleventh centuries).

The nielloing of silver flourished in the town of Veliky Ustiug (Vologda region) beginning with the eighteenth century. The traditions of the old artisans are kept alive by the "Northern Niello", a contemporary factory which puts out elegant silver bracelets. cigarette-cases, toilet boxes, wine-vessels, and other beautiful presentation items embellished with miniature drawings in niello. Niello is a peculiar form of engraving on metal. At first the gold or silver item is subjected to engraving of the ordinary type. The incisions thus produced are then filled with a fused black composition formed of silver, copper, lead and sulphur. Upon heating the powder melts, filling in the cavities of the engraved pattern. After cooling the item is filed and polished, and the nielloed drawing emerges sharp and clear in one of a variety of tones—from pale grey to a velvety black. Not infrequently the decorative effect of the niello pattern is heightened by the addition of gilt engraving. The ineffable forms and the sheer elegance of the niello drawing as set off against the matt glitter of the gold go to make Veliky Ustiug items into art works of the utmost refinement and beauty.

In Soviet times other traditional Russian methods of producing jewelled metalware have also been revived. The "Rostov Enamel" Factory (the city of Rostov Yaroslavsky), organized on the basis of local crafts which historical records date back to at least the 1780s, puts out personal jewellery and souvenirs in enamel. Enamel is a vitrified substance which after burning adheres firmly to metal and has a hard lustrous surface. Painting on enamel is done for the most part with ceramic (fire-resistant) paints. After the decorative painting is applied the item is again subjected to burning.

The painted décor often consists of floral ornaments; the souvenirs, moreover, often carry depictions of landscapes and views of old Russian cities, especially Rostov. A very interesting device is the combination of enamel painting with filigree, which is a dainty openwork pattern of fine twisted silver wires soldered onto a metal carcass.

Filigree and graining, those ancient methods of imparting an artistic aspect to metals, are also widely employed in the jewelcraft of the Krasnoselsky district, where it originated in the late sixteenth and early seventeenth century. The jewellery factories, located in the Krasnoselsky district of the Kostroma region, still use to good effect such ancient metalworking techniques as chasing, engraving and stamping. The openwork filigree, the grain décor and the intricate composition of the factory's small-scale panels, trays and stylized animal figures lend these items a charm all their own and make them into works of Russian decorative and applied art which are truly national in character.

←

72 Wine set. 1972
By Ye. Tropina
The "Northern Niello" Factory, Veliky Ustiug

73 Russian souvenirs. 1974
By Ye. Tropina and V. Shorokhov
The "Northern Niello" Factory, Veliky Ustiug

74 Plate: *Veliky Ustiug*. 1974
By Ye. Tropina
The "Northern Niello" Factory,
Veliky Ustiug

75, 76 Personal ornaments. 1970s
     By A. Khaunov, I. and V. Soldatov, A. Tikhov,
     V. Sharov and V. Zhgariova
     The "Rostov Enamel" Factory,
     Rostov Yaroslavsky

77 Earrings, casket, pendant. 1970s
    By I. and V. Soldatov
    The "Rostov Enamel" Factory,
    Rostov Yaroslavsky

78 Silver necklace. 1970
    By Z. Zenkova

79 Casket in filigree enamel. 1957
    By V. Gorsky
    The "Rostov Enamel" Factory,
    Rostov Yaroslavsky

80 Russian souvenirs:
Warrior, *Horse* and *Bird*. 1972
By N. Gozhev
The Krasnoselskaya Jewellery Factory,
Kostroma region

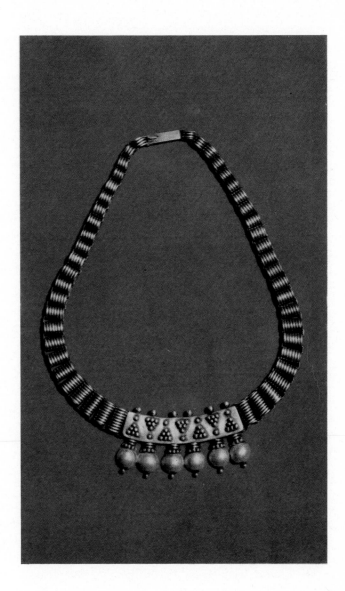

81 Silver necklace. 1967
By M. Toneh

PORCELAIN AND FAIENCE

The first attempts to organize the production of porcelain in Russia go back to the early eighteenth century, but it was only in the middle of that century that the Russian scientist Vinogradov finally found the formula for making porcelain. Today unique items of "Vinogradov" porcelain are the pride of Soviet museums.

The leading role in the production of porcelain ware belongs and has always belonged to the Lomonosov Porcelain Factory in Leningrad. Founded in 1744, it soon evolved into an important cultural centre which was to determine the character of Russian porcelain for the next hundred years.

Leningrad porcelain was always distinguished by the exquisite plasticity of its forms and the subtle restraint of the decorative painting which tended to underscore the properties of the material. The Leningrad tradition is based on the strict style of classicism. Some of the aspects of contemporary items, however, stem from the vivid style of the so-called "propaganda" porcelain of the 1920s. Today the Lomonosov Factory puts out a wide range of items, from technological porcelain for industrial needs to highly artistic pieces which enjoy world repute and have won many gold medals and diplomas at international exhibitions.

The porcelain of the Moscow region differs from the Leningrad product in that it is more colourful, is painted in bright, sweeping brushstrokes, and not least in its forms, which echo the accepted forms of folk applied art. The "Pravda" Porcelain Factory at Duliovo, for example, produces large tea-pots and plates with a painted décor rich in pink, green, red and gold and covering almost the entire surface of each item. The artists of the "Verbilki" Porcelain Factory at Dmitrov have designed many varieties of tableware remarkable for their modern forms and subdued decorative painting.

Faience does not possess the whiteness and transparency of porcelain, but it is nevertheless attractive for the warmth of its glaze, the richness of its texture and the variety of its ornamentation. Dark faience is durable, resistant, solid, and no less beautiful than porcelain.

The Kalinin Faience Factory at Konakovo (Moscow region) produces items characterized by simple forms, a vivid glaze and painstaking finish. The masters involved take folk art for their model, borrowing from it the strictly functional aspect of its wares and the compatibility of the ornamentation with the forms.

82 Vases: "Roses" and "Tulip and Roses". 1970s
By V. Gorodetsky
The Lomonosov Porcelain Factory,
Leningrad

83 Tea-pot "Red Rooster". 1972
By E. Krimmer and A. Vorobyevsky
The Lomonosov Porcelain Factory,
Leningrad

84 Coffee set "Swan". 1973
   By N. Slavina
   The Lomonosov Porcelain Factory, Leningrad

85, 86 Coffee-cups (bone china). 1970s
   By E. Krimmer, L. Lebedinskaya,
   A. Vorobyevsky and N. Guseva
   The Lomonosov Porcelain Factory, Leningrad

87 Coffee set "Promenade" 1973
    By A. Leporskaya and I. Olevskaya
    The Lomonosov Porcelain Factory, Leningrad

→
88 Tea set "Midday". 1969
    By S. Yakovleva and N. Guseva
    The Lomonosov Porcelain Factory,
    Leningrad

89 Tea set "Medallion with Tulip". 1971
By S. Yakovleva and I. Olevskaya
The Lomonosov Porcelain Factory, Leningrad

90 *Fishes.* 1975
By S. Veselov
The Lomonosov Porcelain Factory, Leningrad

91 Porcelain group representing a scene
from A. Ostrovsky's play
Truth Is Fine, But Happiness Is Better. 1973
By N. Malysheva
The "Pravda" Porcelain Factory, Duliovo

92 Coffee set "Sparkles". 1973
By Ye. Smirnov
The Porcelain Factory, Dmitrov

→
93 Tea set "Oak Grove". 1971
By P. Smirnov
The Porcelain Factory, Dmitrov

94 Tea set "Kolobok" 1973
By L. Solodkov
The Kalinin Faience Factory, Konakovo

95 Compote set. 1973
By N. Kokovikhin
The Kalinin Faience Factory, Konakovo

GLASS AND CRYSTAL

The manufacture of glass in Russia is inseparably linked with the name of the eminent Russian scientist Lomonosov. The factory he founded in 1754 near St. Petersburg was the first research laboratory which experimented with different glass-making formulas. Eventually it began producing glass, beads, bugles and mosaic smalts.

Another glass-making factory—St. Petersburg Glassworks, set up also in the eighteenth century—put out unique decorative items for palaces—vases, candelabra, brackets and floor lamps. Working here at one time or another were the most distinguished Russian architects— Voronikhin, Rossi and others—all of whom made brilliant use of glass in interior décor.

A special place in the history of Russian glass belongs to the Gus-Khrustalny Cut-glass Factory (Vladimir region). Founded in the 1750s, it grew into a major glass-producing centre which in the nineteenth century became as much a symbol of Russian crystal as the Baccarat factory for France or Murano glass for Italy. The factory was the first in Russia to produce household items—jugs, flasks, wine-glasses and figured tableware in the shape of birds and animals from green, colourless and semi-transparent glass, much like the free-blown glass of folk tradition. In the second half of the eighteenth century the factory began producing "white glass" tableware with matt engraving, and later on with diamond faceting. The crystal items of the Gus-Khrustalny Factory, inexpensive because made from local raw materials, were superb both in terms of execution and décor. The Gus-Khrustalny Factory of today is one of the largest and most important centres of Soviet glass manufacture with its own laboratories where talented artists model individual items as well as samples for mass production.

The Diatkovo Cut-glass Factory (Briansk region) was founded in the 1790s. Its most popular commodity was cheap glass tableware which was sold all over Russia. Two trends prevail in the factory's output of today: the tradition of diamond faceting is being further developed, and new methods are being sought to decorate items of coloured, colourless and zinc-sulphide glass. Within the framework of Soviet applied art the team of craftsmen of the Leningrad Artistic Glass Factory can be regarded as a distinct school whose salient features are a laconic style, a preference for restrained colours and a never-ending search for new forms and decorative principles. The founder of the Leningrad school was Mukhina, one of the most distinguished Soviet sculptors; in 1940 an experimental workshop was set up on her initiative with the express purpose of finding new, modern forms for glass wares. In 1949 the workshop was reorganized into a factory which during the twenty-five years of its existence has developed into the leading Soviet manufacturer of artistic glass.

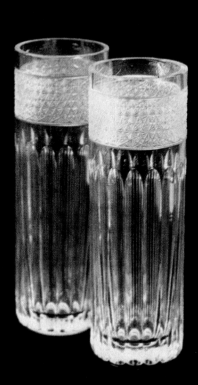

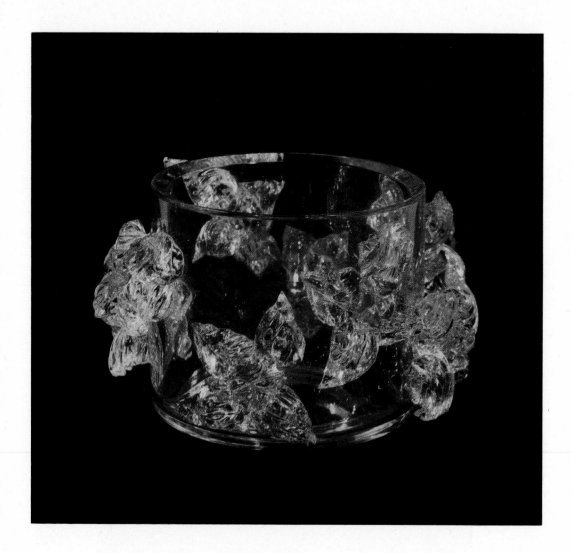

←

96 Vases. 1967
    By V. Shevchenko
    The Diatkovo Cut-glass Factory,
    Briansk region

97 Wine set "Silver Ring". 1967
    By V. Filatov
    The Gus-Khrustalny Cut-glass Factory,
    Vladimir region

98 Vase. 1973
    By S. Pivovarov
    The Gus-Khrustalny Cut-glass Factory,
    Vladimir region

99 Vase. 1972
   By S. Verin
   The Gus-Khrustalny Cut-glass Factory,
   Vladimir region

100 Vase "Waterfall". 1973
   By V. Muratov
   The Gus-Khrustalny Cut-glass Factory,
   Vladimir region

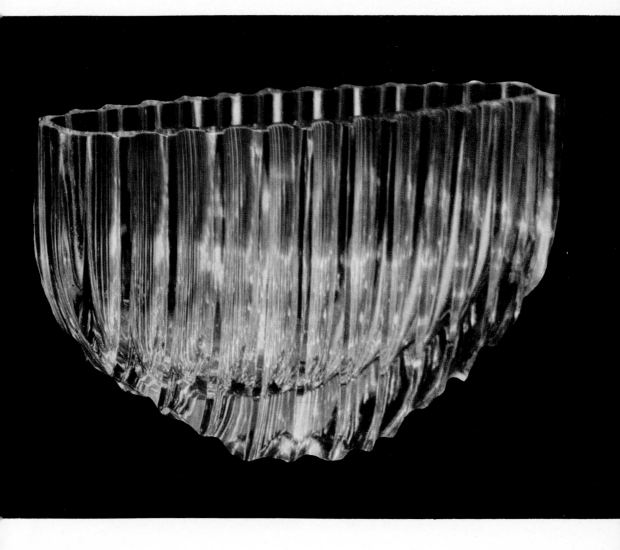

→ 101 Goblet "Lion". 1970
By Ye. Yankovskaya
Artistic Glass Factory, Leningrad

→ 102 "Seamen's Flask". 1967
By Yu. Biakov
Artistic Glass Factory, Leningrad

103 Blown-glass group:
Singing Folk Rhymes. 1973
By I. Marshumova
Glasswork, Kalinin

The works shown in plates
26, 35, 37, 43, 44, 46, 50, 51, 52, 57, 58
are in the Museum of Ethnography
of the Peoples of the USSR, Leningrad.
Whenever available, information about the artists
and their works is given.

The colour reproductions preceding the text show
the Dymkovo clay toy *Turkey-hen*
by Z. Penkina (1971)
and the decorative wall panel *Duliovo*
by A. Brzhezitskaya (1973) produced
at the "Pravda" Porcelain Factory, Duliovo

RUSSIAN SOUVENIRS

Compiled by Maria Chereiskaya
Aurora Art Publishers. Leningrad. 1978

РУССКИЙ СУВЕНИР

Автор-составитель альбома
Мария Григорьевна Черейская
Издательство «Аврора». Ленинград. 1978

Оформление художника Д. М. Плаксина
Фотограф В. А. Стукалов
Перевод с русского Ю. И. Немецкого
Редактор Е. В. Бархатова
Художественный редактор А. Р. Шилов
Редактор английского текста Э. Г. Андреева
Технический редактор Н. А. Зубкова
Корректор И. Н. Стукалина

Сдано в набор 28/IX 1976. Подписано в печать 14/X 1977. Формат 70 × 90/16, бумага мелованная. Усл. печ. л. 9,36. Уч.-изд. л. 10,24. Изд. № 1101. (6-00). Заказ 1443. Издательство «Аврора». 191065, Ленинград, Невский пр., 7/9. Ордена Трудового Красного Знамени ленинградская типография № 3 имени Ивана Федорова Союзполиграфпрома при Государственном комитете Совета Министров СССР по делам издательств, полиграфии и книжной торговли. 196126, Ленинград, Звенигородская ул., 11   ИБ № 595

Printed in the USSR